How to Avoid the Peace

Also by Dave Walker and available from Canterbury Press

The Dave Walker Colouring Book

Heroes of the Coffee Rota

Peculiar Goings On

The Exciting World of Churchgoing

The Dave Walker Guide to the Church

My Pew: Things I Have Seen from It

www.canterburypress.co.uk

How to Avoid the Peace

Tips for Advanced Churchgoing

Dave Walker

CANTERBURY
PRESS
Norwich

© Dave Walker 2017

First published in 2017 by the Canterbury Press Norwich
Editorial office
3rd Floor, Invicta House,
108–114 Golden Lane,
London EC1Y 0TG

Canterbury Press is an imprint of Hymns Ancient & Modern Ltd (a registered charity)
13A Hellesdon Park Road, Norwich,
Norfolk, NR6 5DR, UK

Third impression 2018

www.canterburypress.co.uk

British Library Cataloguing in Publication data

A catalogue record for this book is available
from the British Library

ISBN 978 1 78622 026 4

Typeset by Regent Typesetting
Printed and bound in Great Britain by
CPI Group (UK) Ltd

Thank you to everyone who has helped me with the ideas for these cartoons,
to the Church Times, where these cartoons first appeared,
and to Canterbury Press, for publishing this book.

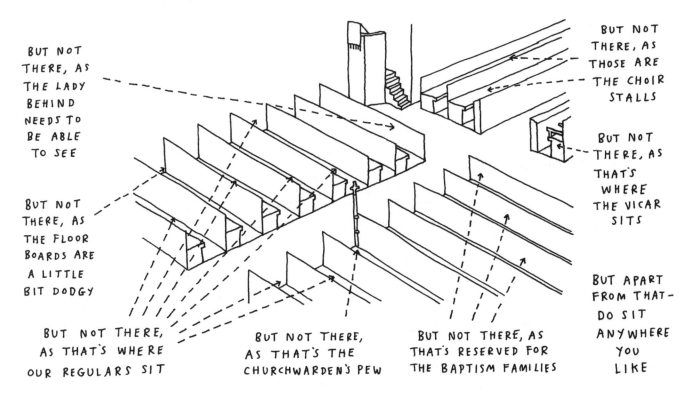

WELCOME

PLEASE SIT ANYWHERE YOU LIKE

BUT NOT THERE, AS THE LADY BEHIND NEEDS TO BE ABLE TO SEE

BUT NOT THERE, AS THE FLOOR BOARDS ARE A LITTLE BIT DODGY

BUT NOT THERE, AS THAT'S WHERE OUR REGULARS SIT

BUT NOT THERE, AS THAT'S THE CHURCHWARDEN'S PEW

BUT NOT THERE, AS THAT'S RESERVED FOR THE BAPTISM FAMILIES

BUT NOT THERE, AS THOSE ARE THE CHOIR STALLS

BUT NOT THERE, AS THAT'S WHERE THE VICAR SITS

BUT APART FROM THAT— DO SIT ANYWHERE YOU LIKE

SECURITY

YOU WILL NEED TO GO THROUGH SECURITY PROCEDURES WHEN YOU ARRIVE FOR THE SERVICE

OUR OFFICERS ARE CHECKING FOR THE FOLLOWING:

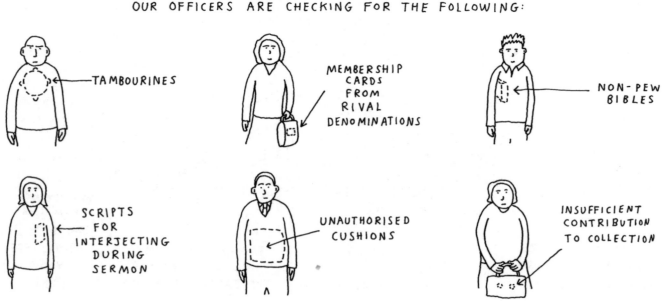

TAMBOURINES

MEMBERSHIP CARDS FROM RIVAL DENOMINATIONS

NON-PEW BIBLES

SCRIPTS FOR INTERJECTING DURING SERMON

UNAUTHORISED CUSHIONS

INSUFFICIENT CONTRIBUTION TO COLLECTION

IN THE PEWS

WHAT IS GOING ON?

WHAT THE VICAR SEES →

ACTUAL ACTIVITIES →

HORTICULTURE   TUNNELING   CROQUET   HOME BREW   RUNNING A SMALL B & B

NO VACANCIES

SUNDAY, 10.30 AM

WHERE THE VICAR NEEDS TO BE

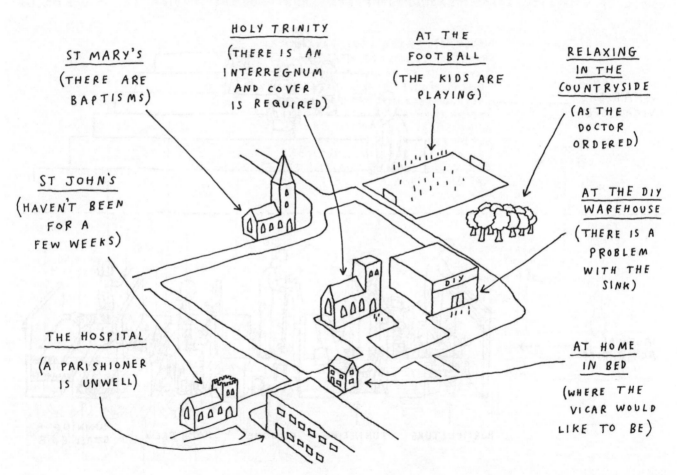

ST MARY'S
(THERE ARE BAPTISMS)

HOLY TRINITY
(THERE IS AN INTERREGNUM AND COVER IS REQUIRED)

AT THE FOOTBALL
(THE KIDS ARE PLAYING)

RELAXING IN THE COUNTRYSIDE
(AS THE DOCTOR ORDERED)

ST JOHN'S
(HAVEN'T BEEN FOR A FEW WEEKS)

AT THE DIY WAREHOUSE
(THERE IS A PROBLEM WITH THE SINK)

THE HOSPITAL
(A PARISHIONER IS UNWELL)

AT HOME IN BED
(WHERE THE VICAR WOULD LIKE TO BE)

WHO DOES WHAT?

HOW RESPONSIBILITIES FOR LEADING DIFFERENT PARTS OF THE SERVICE ARE DIVIDED UP

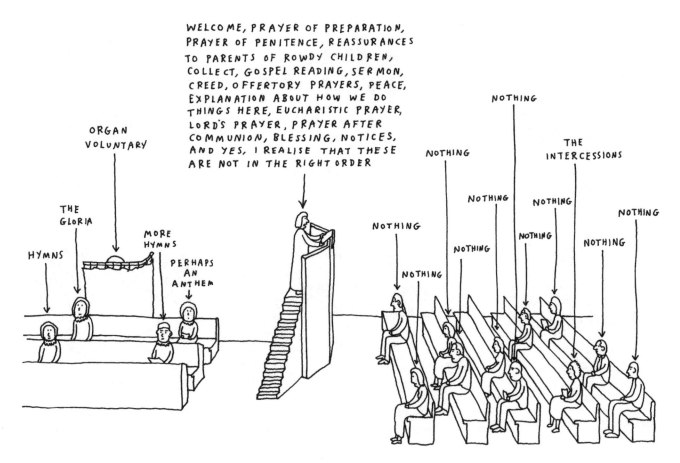

ARRIVING LATE

HOW TO CAUSE MAXIMUM DISRUPTION

DROP 'BRING AND SHARE'
PLATTER AND EXCLAIM LOUDLY

TRY TO PUSH PAST
A PROCESSION

WALK IN THROUGH
THE VESTRY

OBSCURE THE PROJECTOR SCREEN

AT A WEDDING, BURST IN AS 'JUST
IMPEDIMENTS' ARE BEING ASKED FOR

ADOPT THE 'I CAN'T BE SEEN'
CROUCHING POSITION

WORSHIP

HOW TO SPOT WHEN JOLLITY IS BEING ENFORCED

TAMBOURINES, RATTLES, ETC, ETC

A BOX OF INSTRUMENTS IS BROUGHT IN, AND EVERYONE HAS TO PLAY ONE

EVERY MOMENT OF SILENCE IS FILLED WITH SOMEONE PRATTLING ON

SMILES ARE 25% WIDER THAN IS NATURAL

THE CONGREGATION IS SIMPLY INSTRUCTED TO BE HAPPY

7

AUDIENCE PARTICIPATION

WHAT THEY WANT YOU TO DO

TALK TO YOUR
NEIGHBOUR

PUT YOUR
HAND UP

GET INTO
SMALL GROUPS

UNDERTAKE SOME
IMPOSSIBLY COMPLEX TASK

WHAT YOU WILL PROBABLY DO

LOOK
BUSY

RUN
AWAY

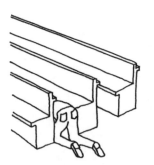

LOOK FOR A HOLE IN THE
GROUND TO CRAWL INTO

GO ALONG WITH THE
WHOLE TEDIOUS RIGMAROLE

MICROPHONES
PEOPLE WHO USE THEM

MY VOICE IS LOUD ENOUGH!

THE SELF-SUFFICIENT

SOUND DESK OPERATOR (DEAFENED)

THE MIC-TAPPER

THE MIC-HOGGER

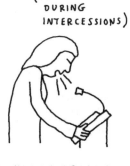

(USUALLY DURING INTERCESSIONS)

THE HEAVY-BREATHER

SCRATCHY STOLE

THE RUSTLER

AM I ON?*

SWITCHED OFF

*NO

THE INEPT

THE SOUL DIVA

UNFAMILIAR LITURGY

THE TAXI COMPANY

9

THE PEACE

HOW TO SPEND THE TIME

CHATTING TO FRIENDS

SAYING HELLO TO PEOPLE ONE HASN'T SEEN IN A WHILE

NETWORKING

NIPPING TO THE LOO

CATCHING UP ON NEWS

CONDUCTING BUSINESS TRANSACTIONS

TRYING TO GET AROUND THE WHOLE CONGREGATION

SWAPPING SPACES ON ROTAS

FEELING RATHER INTIMIDATED BY THE WHOLE SITUATION AND THAT EVERYONE KNOWS EVERYONE ELSE, AND THAT PERHAPS THIS ISN'T THE PLACE FOR ME AFTER ALL

THE PEACE

HOW TO AVOID IT IF IT ISN'T REALLY YOUR SORT OF THING

ADOPT AN
INTIMIDATING
STANCE

LOOK UP THE
NEXT HYMN

FIND
SOME
CHANGE
FOR
THE
COLLECTION

VOLUNTEER
IN THE
KITCHEN

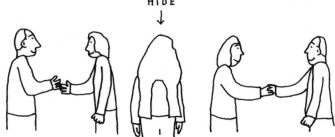

HIDE

FEIGN
AN
INJURY

PREACHERS

WAYS TO MAKE AN OVERENTHUSIASTIC ONE STOP

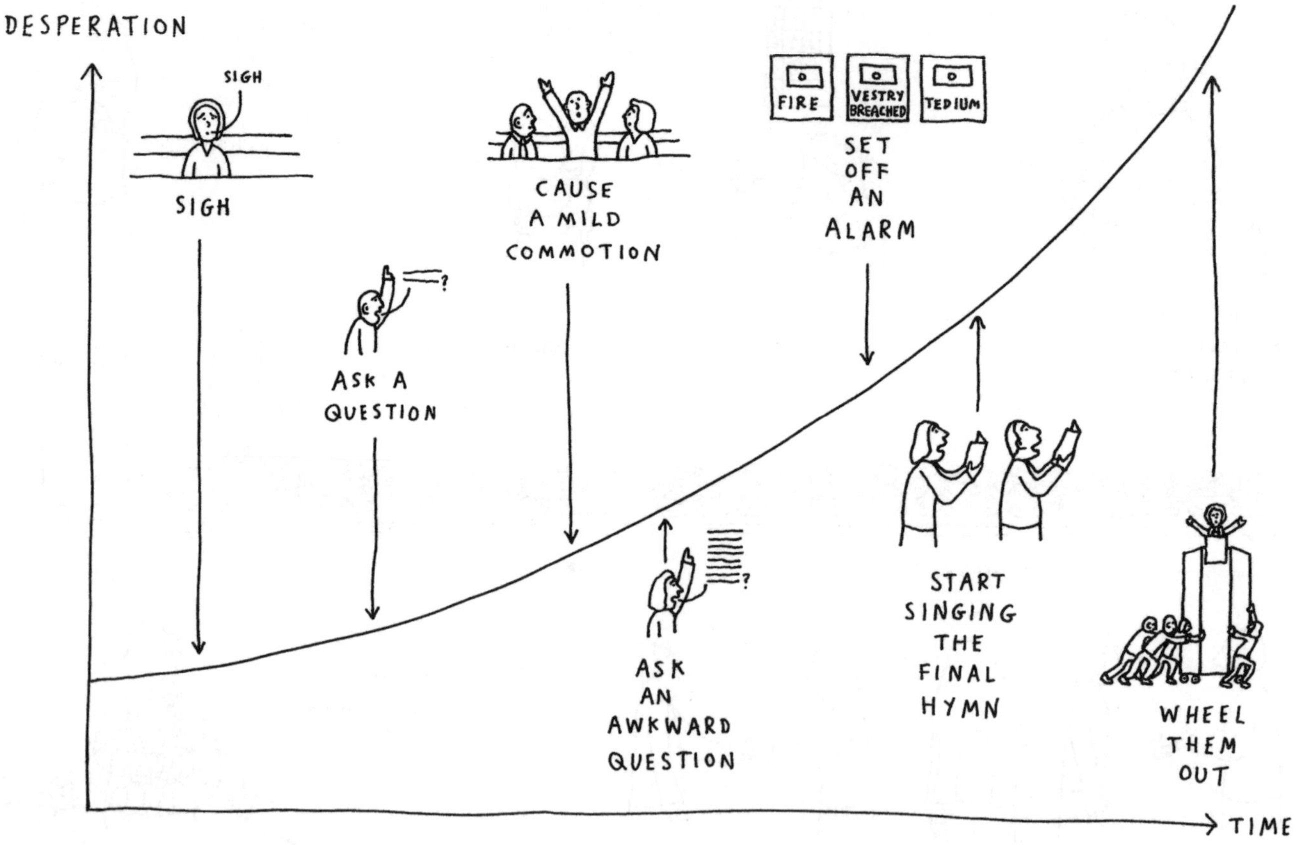
DESPERATION
SIGH
SIGH
CAUSE A MILD COMMOTION
FIRE
VESTRY BREACHED
TEDIUM
SET OFF AN ALARM
?
ASK A QUESTION
?
ASK AN AWKWARD QUESTION
START SINGING THE FINAL HYMN
WHEEL THEM OUT
TIME

THE CELEBRITY SPEAKER

THINGS WE WILL NEED TO DO

CATER FOR THEIR
MEREST WHIM

MAKE SURE THE STAR
FLOWER ARRANGER IS
ON THAT WEEK

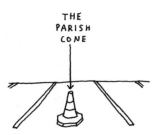

SAVE A
PARKING SPACE

SEE WHETHER THERE IS
A RED CARPET IN
THE NORTH TRANSEPT

FIND A TABLE WITH
EVEN LEGS (FOR
THE BOOK SIGNING)

ENTICE PEOPLE IN
FROM OTHER CHURCHES

PLAN A POST-EVENT
PARTY

CONSIDER CHANGING
THE PULPIT WATER

WASPS

POSSIBLE REACTIONS WHEN ONE APPEARS DURING A SERVICE

COWER

FLAIL

SWAT

IGNORE

PRAY

RUN

THE PROCESSION

OF PEOPLE LEAVING DURING THE SERVICE

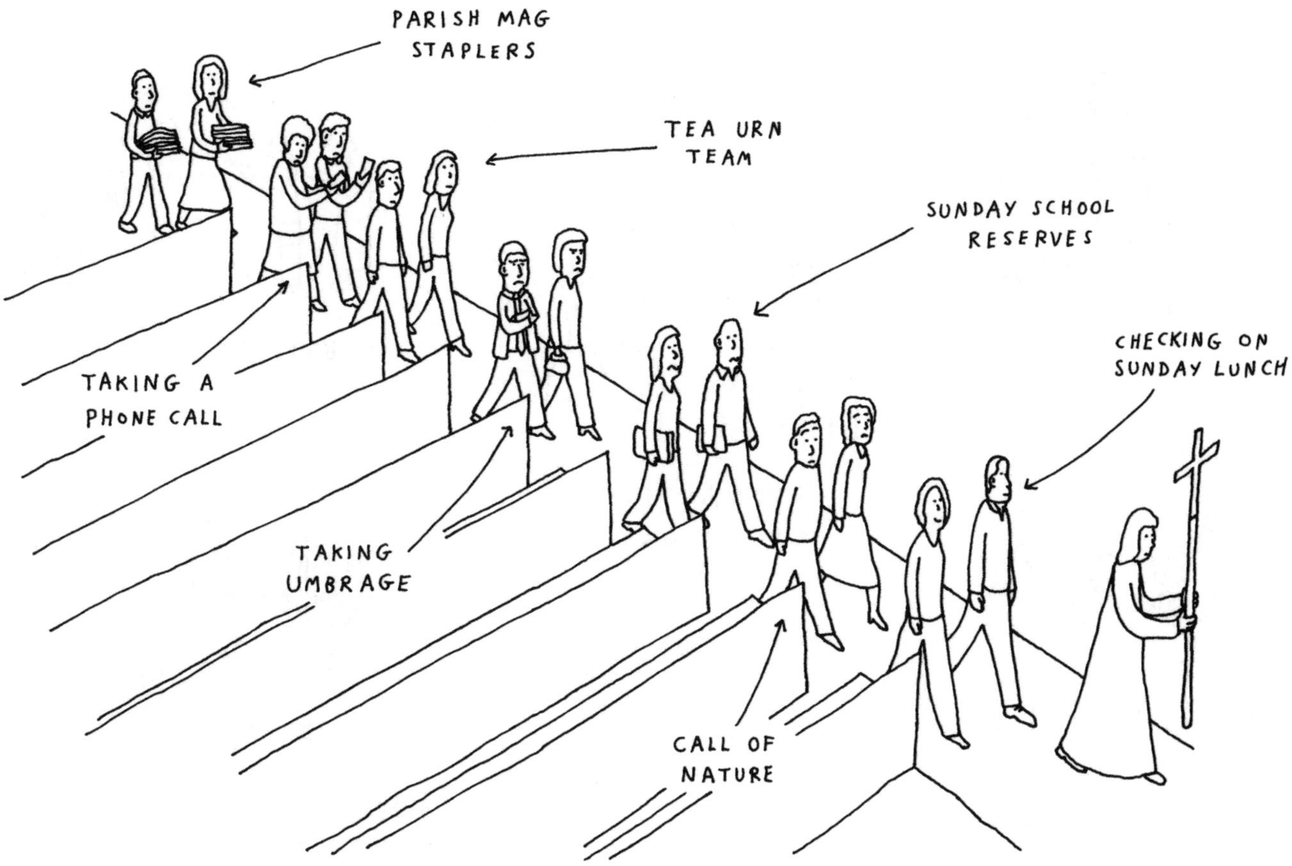
PARISH MAG STAPLERS
TEA URN TEAM
SUNDAY SCHOOL RESERVES
CHECKING ON SUNDAY LUNCH
TAKING A PHONE CALL
TAKING UMBRAGE
CALL OF NATURE

INVITING SOMEONE TO CHURCH

TELL THEM ABOUT THE:

HUGS DURING
THE PEACE

ATTRACTIVE
CHURCHGOERS

BRILLIANT MUSIC

DELICIOUS COFFEE

FREE PRIZES THAT CAN
BE WON IF YOU CORRECTLY
GUESS THE HYMN NUMBERS

PIONEER MINISTERS

THEY GO WHERE OTHER MINISTERS DO NOT DARE TO GO

THEY START CHURCHES WHERE THERE HAS NOT BEEN ONE BEFORE

THEY TAKE RISKS

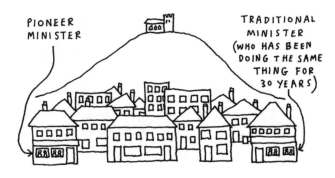

THEY WORK WITH PEOPLE THAT THE TRADITIONAL CHURCH DOES NOT REACH

SCHOOL VISITS TO CHURCH

GUIDELINES FOR CHURCHES

DO A RISK
ASSESSMENT

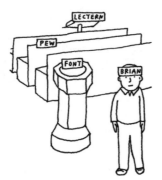

LABEL
EVERYTHING

KNOW HOW TO SPELL
ALL OF THE WORDS

SECURE THE
BUILDING

HAVE AN ANSWER
FOR EVERY 'WHY?'

SUPPLY
REFRESHMENTS

PROVIDE FOR
THE TEACHERS

OFFER INTERESTING
ACTIVITIES

THE TEN WEEK COURSE

FOR NEW CHURCHGOERS

WEEK 1: BASICS OF CHURCH KITCHEN ETIQUETTE

WEEK 2: KEYS. WHO HAS WHICH ONE?

WEEK 3: STANDING/ SITTING/KNEELING MASTERCLASS

WEEK 4: A GUIDE TO HOLDING MULTIPLE BOOKS AND SHEETS OF PAPER

WEEK 5: WASHING UP FOR CHURCH FUNCTIONS (LEVEL 1)

WEEK 6: HOW TO USE THE DEVICE THAT FOLDS THE TABLE LEGS

WEEK 7: STAYING WARM - HINTS AND TIPS

WEEK 8: THE PHOTOCOPIER

WEEK 9: STACKING THE CHAIRS- AN INTRODUCTION TO THE 'S HIGH' RULE

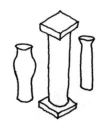

WEEK 10: VASES AND PEDESTALS ORIENTATION

THE HOME GROUP

HOW TO STOP NEW PEOPLE JOINING

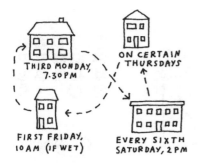

HOLD IT AT DIFFERENT
TIMES IN DIFFERENT PLACES

A LENGTHY APPROVAL
AND AUDITION PROCESS

IGNORE NEWCOMERS AND
MAKE PRIVATE JOKES

ALLOW ONE PERSON TO
DOMINATE THE DISCUSSION

MAKE THE STUDIES
IRRELEVANT

HOLD HANDS WHILST
SINGING HYMNS

THE BAPTISM SERVICE

TIPS FOR CLERGY

MAKE EVERYONE FEEL AT HOME

PREPARE TO SING A SOLO OF THE HYMN THE FAMILY CHOSE

REMOVE FLOWERS FROM THEIR USUAL PLACE IN THE FONT

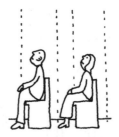

MENTION THE ROOF FUND

TRY TO WORK OUT WHETHER THE CHILD IS A GIRL OR A BOY

KEEP A COPY OF THE LITURGY WITH YOU

GET THE WATER TEMPERATURE RIGHT

REMEMBER EVERYTHING

PERSUADE THE BAPTISM PARTY TO BECOME REGULAR CHURCHGOERS

PREPARE A DARKENED ROOM (TO LIE DOWN IN AFTERWARDS)

21

PASTORAL VISITING

AN A TO Z

AWKWARD SILENCE. ANTICIPATE

BUZZER. MIGHT NOT WORK

CAT/DOG HAIR. APPROPRIATE CLOTHING REQUIRED

DEBRIS. CHECK SOFA

EARPHONES. TAKE OUT

FIRE EXITS. KNOW WHERE THEY ARE

GOOD LISTENER. TRY TO BE ONE

HOUSE NUMBER. MEMORISE

ZIMMER. LEAVE WHERE IT IS

INSIGHTS. OFFER SOME

JESUS. MENTION IF POSSIBLE

YESTERDAY. DON'T APPEAR A DAY LATE

MON 17th

KIDS/FAMILY? WAY TO BREAK THE ICE

XYLOPHONE. DON'T STEP ON KIDS' TOYS

LOO. TRY NOT TO NEED

WALLPAPER. MAKE NO COMMENT

MINCE PIE. ACCEPT

VALUABLES. TRY NOT TO BREAK ANY

NAMES. REMEMBER THEM

UPSTAIRS. DON'T GO

OVERSTAYING WELCOME. AVOID

TEA. LEARN TO DRINK THE COFFEE YOU'RE GIVEN

SHOES. OFFER TO REMOVE

RADIO/TV. COPE IF LEFT ON

QUEASINESS. STICK TO ONE SLICE OF CAKE

PRAYER BOOK. TAKE IT WITH YOU

CASSOCKS
BECOME UNEXPECTEDLY POPULAR

AT THE SUPERMARKET

AT THE FOOTBALL MATCH

AT THE GYM

EVEN AT THE DISCOTHEQUE

23

FORMS

THE CLERGY MUST FILL THEM IN

THESE ARE THE FORMS THAT
MUST BE COMPLETED

FORM-FILLING
REFRESHMENT.
MAY NOT HELP.
PROBABLY
WON'T HINDER

MANY LATE NIGHTS IN THE
STUDY WILL BE REQUIRED

Q26(c) WHAT COULD YOU
ACHIEVE IF YOU DIDN'T
HAVE TO FILL IN ALL
OF THESE FORMS?

EXAMPLE OF FORM

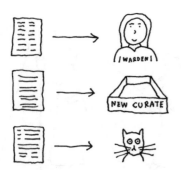

IF POSSIBLE TRY TO PASS
SOME OF THEM TO OTHERS

BUT DON'T DESPAIR. THE
DIOCESE CAN HELP

(PLEASE FILL IN THE FEEDBACK
FORM AFTERWARDS)

WHERE ARE MY KEYS?

A GUIDE FOR CLERGY AND CHURCH OFFICIALS

IN THE VICARAGE DOOR

IN THE FONT

IN THE CAR

ON THE PHOTOCOPIER

IN THE PULPIT

IN THE BIN

IN THE PUB

UNDER A PEW

IN THE CHURCH THAT HELD DEANERY SYNOD

ON THE HOOK

ON THE SOFA OF THE BAPTISM FAMILY

IN THE SAFE

IN THE DOG'S BASKET

UP THE TOWER

IN THE CHILDREN'S MUSICAL INSTRUMENTS BOX

WERE THERE EVER REALLY ANY KEYS?

IN YESTERDAY'S CASSOCK

WHEREVER YOU LAST SAW THEM

25

THE NEW CURATE

JOBS TO KEEP THEM OCCUPIED DURING THEIR FIRST WEEK

CONDUCTING A DOOR-TO-DOOR
SURVEY OF THE ENTIRE PARISH

UPDATING THE
CONTACTS DATABASE

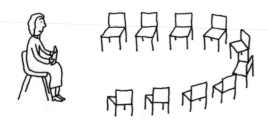

STARTING A SUNDAY SCHOOL
AND A YOUTH CLUB

CLEARING OUT THE
NORTH TRANSEPT

NEW CURATES

THEIR TASKS

ORGANISING BOOKS OVERZEALOUSLY
BOUGHT AT THEOLOGICAL COLLEGE

RECEIVING KEYS TO ALL
OF THE CHURCHES

GETTING TO GRIPS WITH
THE PHOTOCOPIER

REMEMBERING A LOT
OF NAMES

GETTING USED TO REACTIONS
TO THE DOG COLLAR

CHANGING
THE WORLD

#NEWREVS

SUPPLY CLERGY

WHEN CONGREGATIONS MISBEHAVE

HOLDING THE DOOR SHUT

"WE HAD THESE READINGS LAST WEEK"

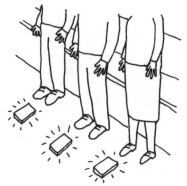

ALL DROPPING HYMN BOOKS AT THE SAME TIME

"WE DON'T HAVE A VESTRY"

MUMBLING THE HYMNS

SITTING IN THE WRONG PEWS

THE VICAR'S CAMERA

SELECTED PHOTOGRAPHS

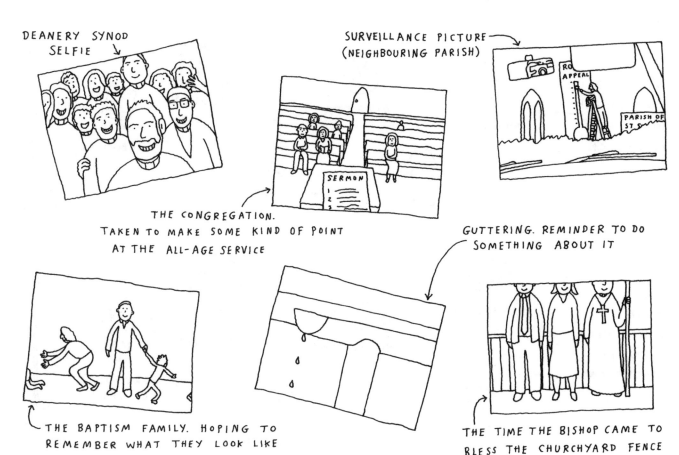

DEANERY SYNOD SELFIE

SURVEILLANCE PICTURE (NEIGHBOURING PARISH)

THE CONGREGATION. TAKEN TO MAKE SOME KIND OF POINT AT THE ALL-AGE SERVICE

GUTTERING. REMINDER TO DO SOMETHING ABOUT IT

THE BAPTISM FAMILY. HOPING TO REMEMBER WHAT THEY LOOK LIKE

THE TIME THE BISHOP CAME TO BLESS THE CHURCHYARD FENCE

LEFT BEHIND

IN THE VESTRY CUPBOARD WHEN CLERGY LEAVE THE PARISH

WHEN THE
HIGH CHURCH →
INCUMBENT
MOVES ON

THURIBLE

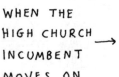
BIRETTA

COTTA

MONSTRANCE

CANDLES

IRREGULAR
LITURGY

GOLF
CLUB

WHEN THE
LOW CHURCH →
INCUMBENT
MOVES ON

TAMBOURINE

PROJECTOR

STUDY BIBLE

GUITAR STRAP

DOCTRINAL
STATEMENT

IRREGULAR
LITURGY

GOLF
CLUB

THE INTERREGNUM

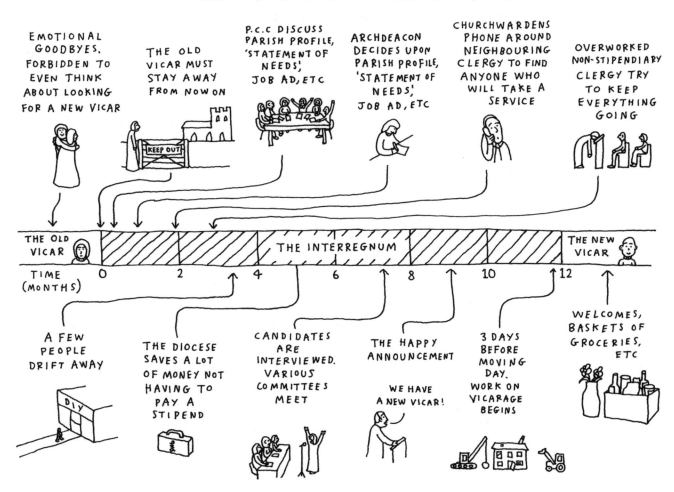

EMOTIONAL GOODBYES, FORBIDDEN TO EVEN THINK ABOUT LOOKING FOR A NEW VICAR

THE OLD VICAR MUST STAY AWAY FROM NOW ON

P.C.C DISCUSS PARISH PROFILE, 'STATEMENT OF NEEDS', JOB AD, ETC

ARCHDEACON DECIDES UPON PARISH PROFILE, 'STATEMENT OF NEEDS', JOB AD, ETC

CHURCHWARDENS PHONE AROUND NEIGHBOURING CLERGY TO FIND ANYONE WHO WILL TAKE A SERVICE

OVERWORKED NON-STIPENDIARY CLERGY TRY TO KEEP EVERYTHING GOING

KEEP OUT

THE OLD VICAR

THE INTERREGNUM

THE NEW VICAR

TIME (MONTHS)   0   2   4   6   8   10   12

A FEW PEOPLE DRIFT AWAY

DIY

THE DIOCESE SAVES A LOT OF MONEY NOT HAVING TO PAY A STIPEND

CANDIDATES ARE INTERVIEWED. VARIOUS COMMITTEES MEET

THE HAPPY ANNOUNCEMENT

WE HAVE A NEW VICAR!

3 DAYS BEFORE MOVING DAY. WORK ON VICARAGE BEGINS

WELCOMES, BASKETS OF GROCERIES, ETC

COMMITTEES

A TYPICAL STRUCTURE

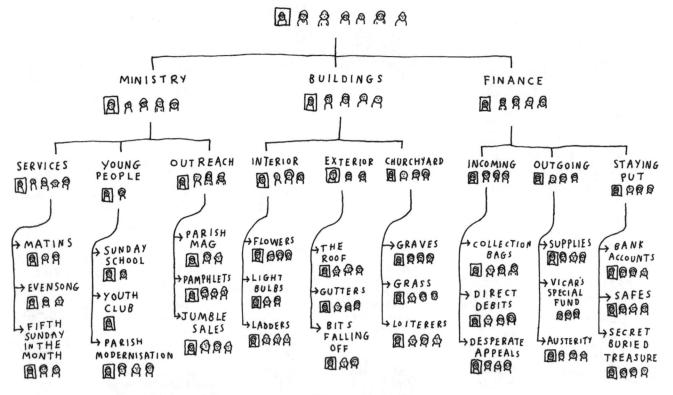

THE PAROCHIAL CHURCH COUNCIL

MINISTRY   BUILDINGS   FINANCE

SERVICES   YOUNG PEOPLE   OUTREACH   INTERIOR   EXTERIOR   CHURCHYARD   INCOMING   OUTGOING   STAYING PUT

→ MATINS

→ EVENSONG

→ FIFTH SUNDAY IN THE MONTH

→ SUNDAY SCHOOL

→ YOUTH CLUB

→ PARISH MODERNISATION

→ PARISH MAG

→ PAMPHLETS

→ JUMBLE SALES

→ FLOWERS

→ LIGHT BULBS

→ LADDERS

→ THE ROOF

→ GUTTERS

→ BITS FALLING OFF

→ GRAVES

→ GRASS

→ LOITERERS

→ COLLECTION BAGS

→ DIRECT DEBITS

→ DESPERATE APPEALS

→ SUPPLIES

→ VICAR'S SPECIAL FUND

→ AUSTERITY

→ BANK ACCOUNTS

→ SAFES

→ SECRET BURIED TREASURE

KEY: THE VICAR

32

THE P.C.C.

NEEDS A
MONDAY EVENING
ACTIVITY

IT'S
MY
JOB

TOKEN
YOUNG PERSON
(MID 40 S)

GLASS
HALF
FULL

GLASS
HALF
EMPTY

NEEDS
NEW
GLASSES

NEWLY APPOINTED,
INCREDIBLY KEEN

SEEN IT
ALL

COMPLETELY
SILENT

CAN'T
HEAR

WON'T
HEAR

NOT
HERE

MAKING SURE
OF SCHOOL
PLACES

ASKS QUESTIONS ON
POINTS EXPLAINED
TWO MINUTES AGO

WE SHOULD
SPEND ALL
OF THE MONEY

WE REALLY
CAN'T AFFORD
IT

BRINGER OF INSIGHTS
FROM THE WORLD
OF BUSINESS

BRINGER
OF
FLAPJACKS

33

THE P.C.C. MEETING

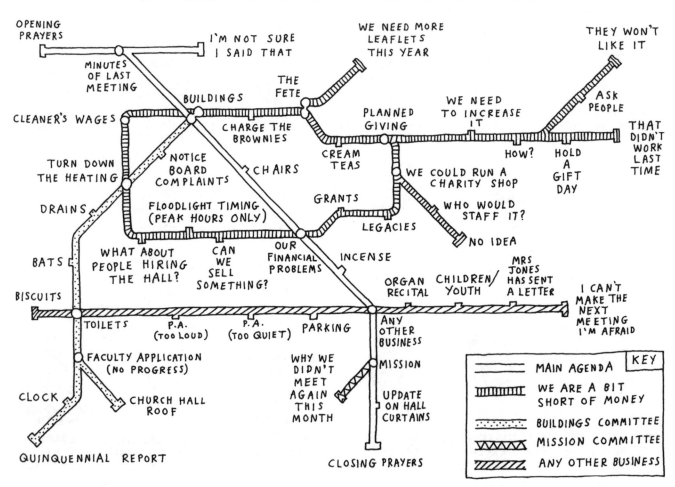

OPENING PRAYERS

MINUTES OF LAST MEETING

I'M NOT SURE I SAID THAT

WE NEED MORE LEAFLETS THIS YEAR

THEY WON'T LIKE IT

BUILDINGS

THE FETE

PLANNED GIVING

WE NEED TO INCREASE IT

ASK PEOPLE

CLEANER'S WAGES

CHARGE THE BROWNIES

CREAM TEAS

HOW?

HOLD A GIFT DAY

THAT DIDN'T WORK LAST TIME

TURN DOWN THE HEATING

NOTICE BOARD COMPLAINTS

CHAIRS

WE COULD RUN A CHARITY SHOP

DRAINS

FLOODLIGHT TIMING (PEAK HOURS ONLY)

GRANTS

WHO WOULD STAFF IT?

LEGACIES

NO IDEA

BATS

WHAT ABOUT PEOPLE HIRING THE HALL?

CAN WE SELL SOMETHING?

OUR FINANCIAL PROBLEMS

INCENSE

ORGAN RECITAL

CHILDREN/ YOUTH

MRS JONES HAS SENT A LETTER

BISCUITS

I CAN'T MAKE THE NEXT MEETING I'M AFRAID

TOILETS

P.A. (TOO LOUD)

P.A. (TOO QUIET)

PARKING

ANY OTHER BUSINESS

FACULTY APPLICATION (NO PROGRESS)

WHY WE DIDN'T MEET AGAIN THIS MONTH

MISSION

CLOCK

CHURCH HALL ROOF

UPDATE ON HALL CURTAINS

QUINQUENNIAL REPORT

CLOSING PRAYERS

KEY

——	MAIN AGENDA
▥▥▥	WE ARE A BIT SHORT OF MONEY
⋯⋯	BUILDINGS COMMITTEE
∨∨∨	MISSION COMMITTEE
⫽⫽⫽	ANY OTHER BUSINESS

THE HUSTINGS

POTENTIAL PAROCHIAL CHURCH COUNCIL MEMBERS EXPLAIN THEIR POLICIES

THE ECONOMY

HOW CAN WE RAISE THE MONEY FOR THE PARISH SHARE?

A TIME OF AUSTERITY IS NEEDED. WE COULD SELL THE CHURCH HALL

WE MUST PRODUCE A NEW 'PLANNED GIVING' LEAFLET

BIGGER COLLECTION PLATES

EDUCATION

WHAT'S YOUR VIEW ON THE SUNDAY SCHOOL?

WE NEED A RADICAL SHAKEUP OF THE ROTA

INCREASE THE BUDGET (MORE GLITTER)

FREE BISCUITS

THE ENVIRONMENT

WHAT IS YOUR VISION FOR THE CHURCHYARD?

I THINK WE SHOULD EXPLORE THE FRACKING POTENTIAL

LET IT GO BACK TO NATURE (MOWER IS BROKEN)

INVEST IN RECYCLING (GET A NEW BIN)

IMMIGRATION

SHOULD WE WELCOME REFUGEES FROM OTHER CHURCHES?

NO. THEY ARE TAKING OUR PEWS AND DRINKING OUR COFFEE

YES. BECAUSE WE ALL GO ELSEWHERE WHEN IT'S OUR FAMILY SERVICE

ONLY IF THEY JOIN A ROTA

P.C.C. PAPERWORK

THREE WAYS TO STORE IT

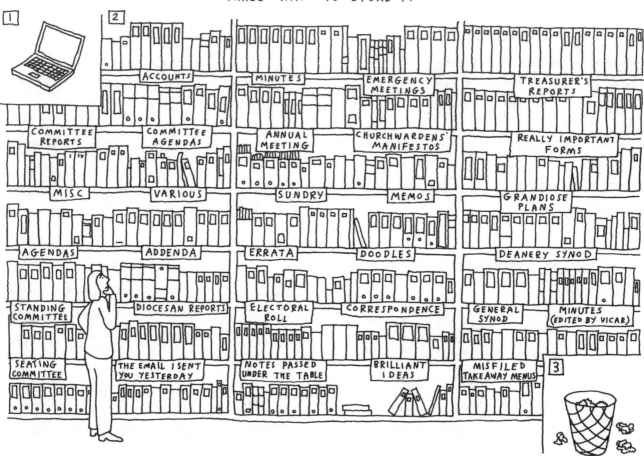

GIVING

WHY I DO NOT CONTRIBUTE

THE CHURCH
HAS PLENTY
OF MONEY

WE CAN'T
AFFORD
IT

I GIVE MY TIME
AND TALENTS
INSTEAD

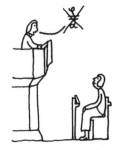

CHURCH ISN'T
THE PLACE TO
TALK ABOUT MONEY

DOESN'T THE
GOVERNMENT
PAY FOR IT?

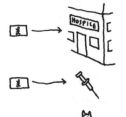

I GIVE
TO OTHER
CHARITIES

WHAT I COULD
GIVE WOULDN'T MAKE
A DIFFERENCE

THE MONEY
WON'T BE
WELL-SPENT

OUR VICAR
DOESN'T DESERVE
TO BE PAID

SOMEBODY
UPSET
ME ONCE

GIFT AID

HOW YOUR CHURCH CAN CLAIM GIFT AID ON SMALL DONATIONS GIVEN BY PEOPLE WHO HAVEN'T FILLED IN A FORM. (THE 'GIFT AIDED SMALL DONATIONS SCHEME')

KEY: ✓ CAN CLAIM GIFT AID
      ✗ CANNOT CLAIM GIFT AID

 CASH ✓

 CHEQUE ✗

 TEXT ✗

 £30 IN CASH ✓

(WE DON'T KNOW WHO GAVE WHICH NOTES)

 £30 CASH IN AN ENVELOPE ✗

(BECAUSE IT IS CLEARLY FROM ONE PERSON AND OVER £20 LIMIT)

(LIMIT OF £20 PER PERSON AND EACH MUST GIVE THEIR OWN)

 £50 NOTE ✗

(BECAUSE A £50 NOTE IS MORE THAN £20)

STEVE STAYED IN BED ✗

(THERE MUST BE AT LEAST TEN PEOPLE PRESENT)

EVERYONE WATCHING? ✓

(TEN PEOPLE ARE PRESENT)

 ✗

DONATIONS FOR REFRESHMENTS

(DONORS CANNOT RECEIVE ANY BENEFIT FROM THEIR DONATIONS)

DISCLAIMERS   1) THIS IS NOT FINANCIAL ADVICE   2) IT IS COMPLICATED   3) I AM SLIGHTLY BAFFLED

CREDIT UNIONS

CHURCHES MAKE THEIR FIRST FORAYS INTO BANKING

CASHBACK
DURING SERVICES

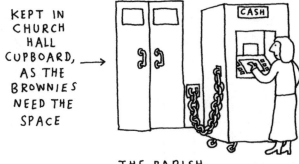

KEPT IN
CHURCH
HALL
CUPBOARD, →
AS THE
BROWNIES
NEED THE
SPACE

THE PARISH
CASH MACHINE

APPLY FOR
A LOAN

MARJORIE'S
LASAGNE
DISH

LOANS TO
PARISHIONERS

THE PEACE
(CONTACTLESS)

39

REORDERING YOUR CHURCH

HOW TO DO IT WITHOUT ANYONE NOTICING

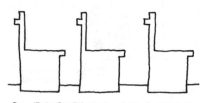

DO EVERYTHING AT A TIME
WHEN NO ONE WILL BE AROUND

KEEP PEOPLE AWAY

CARRY OUT THE WORK GRADUALLY

DISGUISE ALL EQUIPMENT

FOAM
PADDING

MODIFY TOOLS TO REDUCE NOISE

GRIND PEWS INTO SAWDUST
AND RELEASE SURREPTITIOUSLY

THE CHURCH EXTENSION

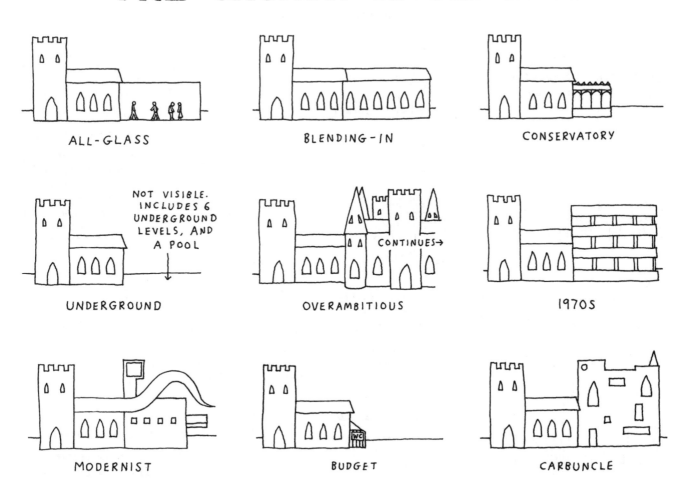

ALL-GLASS

BLENDING-IN

CONSERVATORY

UNDERGROUND

NOT VISIBLE. INCLUDES 6 UNDERGROUND LEVELS, AND A POOL

OVERAMBITIOUS

CONTINUES→

1970S

MODERNIST

BUDGET

WC

CARBUNCLE

APPLYING FOR A FACULTY

THE PEOPLE INVOLVED

THE CONGREGATION
(HAVE BEEN DRIPPED-UPON
FOR SOME TIME NOW)

FLAK
JACKET

THE VICAR
AND P.C.C

THE ARCHITECT
(HAS DEVISED
A GRANDIOSE
SCHEME)

EXPLANATION
A 'FACULTY' IS A
LICENCE REQUIRED
FOR ALL REPAIRS,
ALTERATIONS, OR
PLANS TO MOVE
ANYTHING A
COUPLE OF INCHES
FROM A TO B,
WITHIN
A CHURCH

THE NEIGHBOURS
(ATTEND EVERY OTHER
CHRISTMAS.
VEHEMENTLY OPPOSED)

THE 'KEEP EVERYTHING
THE SAME' SOCIETY
(THEY WOULD LIKE
EVERYTHING TO BE
KEPT THE SAME)

THE FUNDRAISING
COMMITTEE
(MUST RAISE THE
MONEY USING
RESOURCES AVAILABLE)

SOME
DONATED →
TOILETRIES

LAWYERS

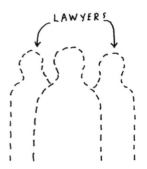

THE ARCHDEACON
(I CAN'T REMEMBER WHAT
THEY DO, BUT IT IS
TERRIBLY IMPORTANT)

THE DIOCESAN AUTHORITIES
(SHROUDED IN MYSTERY.
ALMOST CERTAINLY WEAR SHADES)

DECORATING

THE VESTRY

THE VESTRY-DECORATION SUBCOMMITTEE
CONSIDERS PREFERRED SHADES AND PATTERNS

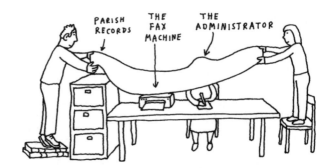

DUST SHEETS ARE PLACED OVER THE VALUABLES

EQUIPMENT IS GATHERED,
AND THE WORK COMMENCES

A FEW WEEKS LATER: THE FINISHED
RESULT IS REVEALED

THE CHURCH HALL

CONDITIONS OF HIRE

FILL IN THE PAPERWORK

ARRIVE AND LEAVE QUIETLY

DON'T CRAM TOO MANY PEOPLE IN

DON'T STICK ANYTHING ON THE WALLS

STACK THE CHAIRS AS YOU FOUND THEM

CLEAN EVERYTHING UP

CHURCH NOTICE BOARDS

THE SEVEN DEADLY SINS

WRATH (DIRECTED AT INVALID ADDITIONS)

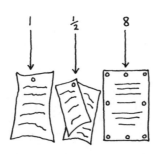

GREED (USING TOO MANY OF THE PARISH PINS)

SLOTH (NOT REMOVING OLD NOTICES)

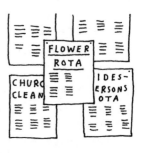

PRIDE (COVERING UP OTHERS' WORK)

LUST (COVETING THY NEIGHBOUR'S FONT, LAYOUT, ETC)

ENVY (RIVAL CHURCHES POACHING OUR CONGREGATION)

GLUTTONY (OVERINDULGENCE, ETC)

THE GRAVEYARD

THINGS YOU MIGHT FIND

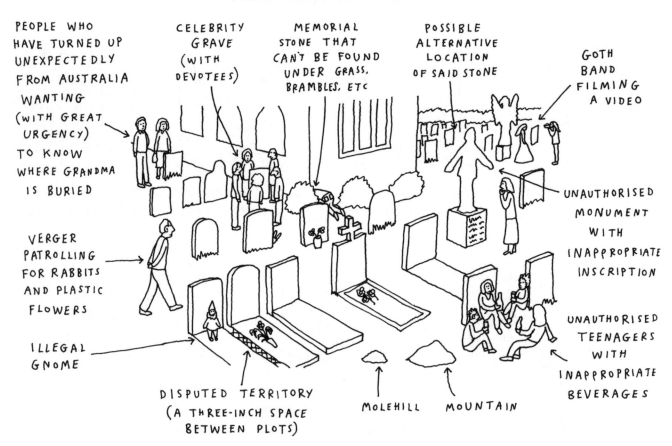

PEOPLE WHO HAVE TURNED UP UNEXPECTEDLY FROM AUSTRALIA WANTING (WITH GREAT URGENCY) TO KNOW WHERE GRANDMA IS BURIED

CELEBRITY GRAVE (WITH DEVOTEES)

MEMORIAL STONE THAT CAN'T BE FOUND UNDER GRASS, BRAMBLES, ETC

POSSIBLE ALTERNATIVE LOCATION OF SAID STONE

GOTH BAND FILMING A VIDEO

VERGER PATROLLING FOR RABBITS AND PLASTIC FLOWERS

ILLEGAL GNOME

UNAUTHORISED MONUMENT WITH INAPPROPRIATE INSCRIPTION

UNAUTHORISED TEENAGERS WITH INAPPROPRIATE BEVERAGES

DISPUTED TERRITORY (A THREE-INCH SPACE BETWEEN PLOTS)

MOLEHILL   MOUNTAIN

THE CHURCHYARD

THOSE ON THE MOWING ROTA, AND THEIR PREFERRED APPROACH

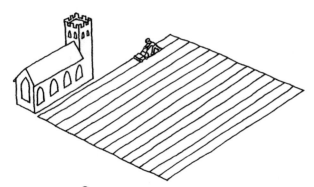

 BOB: MANICURED

CHRIS: MAZE

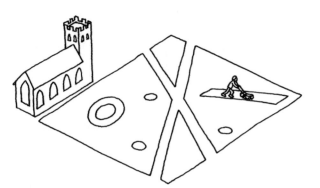

PHIL: ARTISTIC

JIM: FORGETS, GOES TO PUB

THE SKIP

DECIDING WHAT CAN GO IN IT

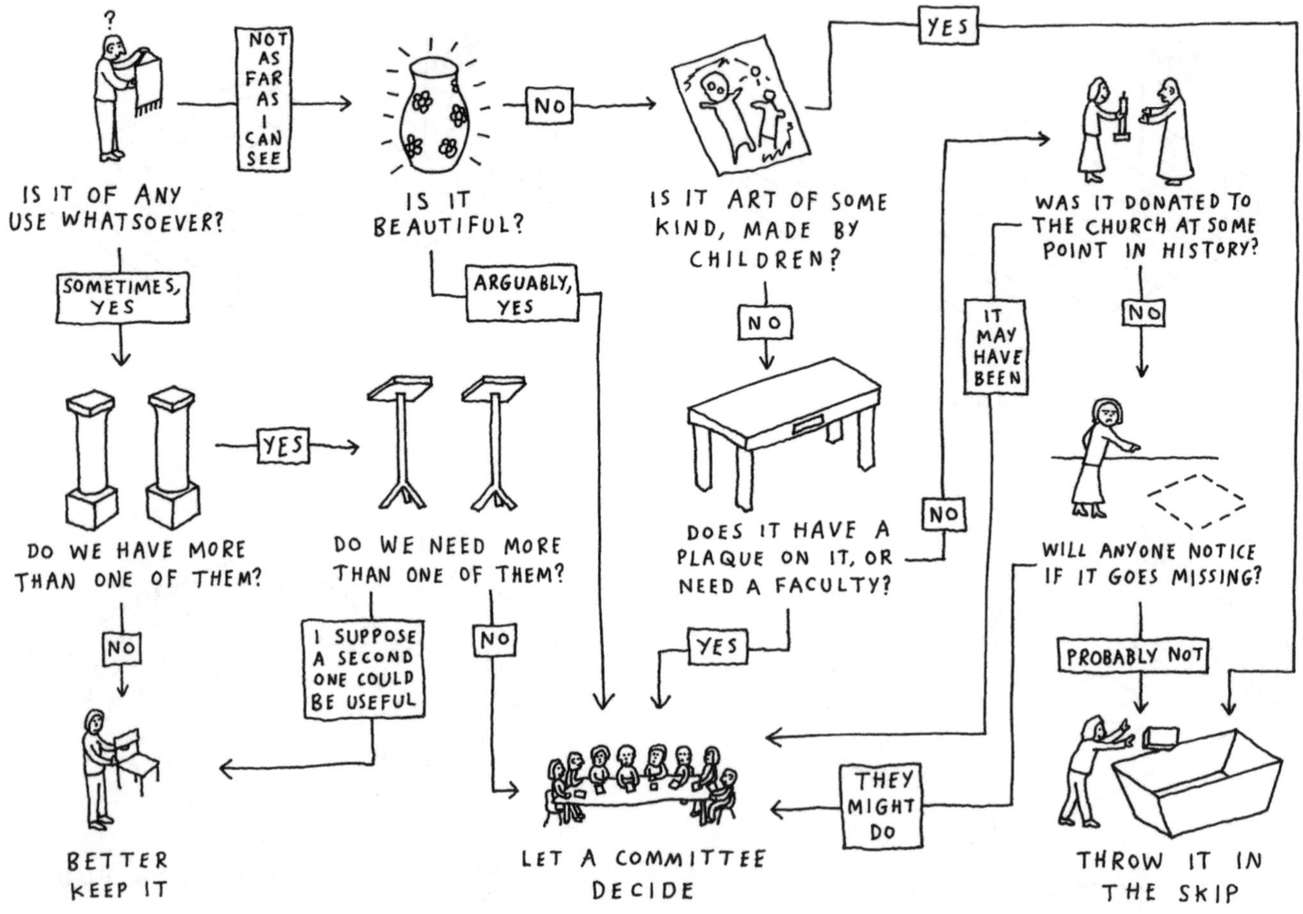

?
IS IT OF ANY USE WHATSOEVER?
NOT AS FAR AS I CAN SEE
IS IT BEAUTIFUL?
NO
IS IT ART OF SOME KIND, MADE BY CHILDREN?
YES
WAS IT DONATED TO THE CHURCH AT SOME POINT IN HISTORY?
SOMETIMES, YES
ARGUABLY, YES
NO
IT MAY HAVE BEEN
NO
DO WE HAVE MORE THAN ONE OF THEM?
YES
DO WE NEED MORE THAN ONE OF THEM?
DOES IT HAVE A PLAQUE ON IT, OR NEED A FACULTY?
NO
WILL ANYONE NOTICE IF IT GOES MISSING?
NO
I SUPPOSE A SECOND ONE COULD BE USEFUL
NO
YES
PROBABLY NOT
THEY MIGHT DO
BETTER KEEP IT
LET A COMMITTEE DECIDE
THROW IT IN THE SKIP

BRASS

THE BRASS CLEANERS

THEY ARE THE CUSTODIANS
OF OUR CHURCH BRASS

SPRAYS

POLISHES

RUBBING REGS

CLOTHS

RULES

CONES

OUR CHURCH BRASS POLICY

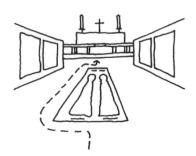

SIDESTEP THE
MONUMENTAL BRASSES

WEAR READING GLOVES
AT THE LECTERN

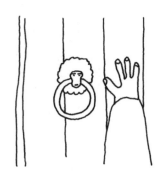

AVOID USING THE
DOOR HANDLE

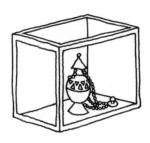

THE THURIBLE MUST
REMAIN IN ITS CABINET

INSPECTIONS

THESE MUST BE CARRIED OUT REGULARLY

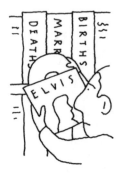

RECORDS

REGISTERS

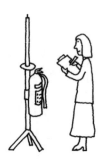

EXTINGUISHERS

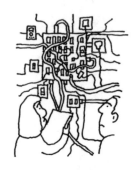

WIRING

ACCOUNTS

PORTABLE CHURCH APPLIANCE TESTING

PRE-SERVICE CHECKS

THE PRAYER BOARD

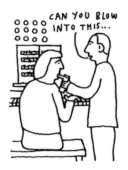

THE ORGANIST

DROOP

SACRED ITEMS

INSTRUCTIONS FOR USE

PLEASE DO NOT MOVE
THE PORTABLE LECTERN

WALKING ON THE NEW
CARPET IS FORBIDDEN

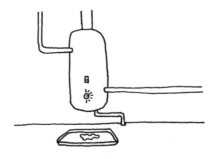

LEAVE THIS TRAY UNDER THE
BOILER TO CATCH DRIPS

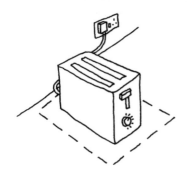

THE CHURCH KITCHEN TOASTER
MUST REMAIN WITHIN THESE LINES

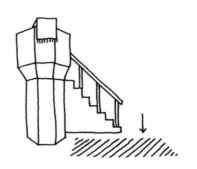

THE NATIVITY CAN ONLY BE
PLACED IN THIS SPOT

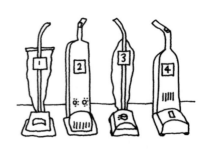

THIS IS HOW WE PARK
THE VACUUM CLEANERS

THE FLOWER ARRANGERS

CAREER PROGRESSION

DEMOTION ← → PROMOTION

TINY WINDOW IN THE BROOM CUPBOARD

ON THE VICAR'S DESK

SMALL WINDOW

GRANDIOSE WINDOW

LARGE DISPLAY IN THE CHANCEL

LOFTY TASKS

CAN NEW TECHNOLOGY REPLACE TRADITIONAL METHODS?

TASK → / TECHNOLOGY ↓	CHANGING LIGHT BULBS	CHECKING FOR BROKEN ROOF TILES	DUSTING GARGOYLES	DEALING WITH PIGEONS IN THE TOWER	DELIVERING HYMN BOOKS
DRONE	LACKS OPPOSABLE THUMBS	ENTIRELY COMPETENT	3/10	PIGEONS: 1 DRONE: NIL	INDISCRIMINATE
CHURCHWARDEN ON LADDER	THE TIME-HONOURED METHOD	SAFETY CONCERNS	7/10	THEY WILL KNOW WHAT TO DO	TARGETED (LADDER PERHAPS UNNECESSARY)

CONCLUSION: FOR MOST TASKS STICK WITH CHURCHWARDENS, AND/OR DEVELOP SOME KIND OF CHURCHWARDEN-DRONE

53

THE PROJECTOR

A SACRED OFFICE: THE CHANGING OF THE BULB

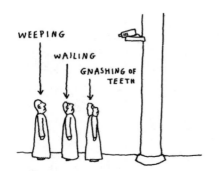

WEEPING

WAILING

GNASHING OF TEETH

IT IS DISCOVERED THAT THE BULB HAS EXPIRED

THE BOX IS CAREFULLY PROCESSED DOWN THE AISLE

WORDS FROM THE INSTRUCTION BOOK ARE RECITED

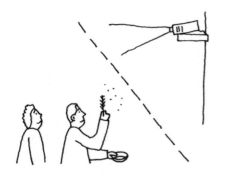

THE LAMP IS BLESSED AS IT IS SWITCHED ON FOR THE FIRST TIME

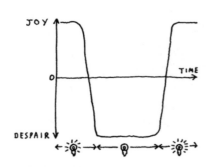

THE MINISTERS DEPART, REJOICING

THE OFFICE IS REPEATED AFTER ANOTHER 1250 HOURS OF USE

THE VERGER'S OFFICE

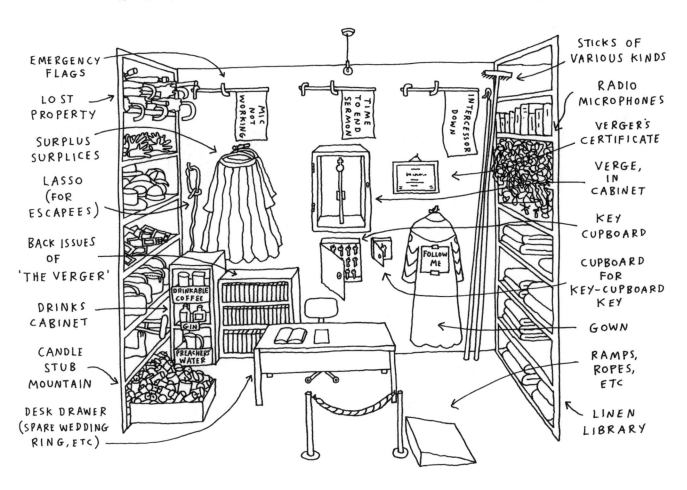

EMERGENCY FLAGS

LOST PROPERTY

SURPLUS SURPLICES

LASSO (FOR ESCAPEES)

BACK ISSUES OF 'THE VERGER'

DRINKS CABINET

CANDLE STUB MOUNTAIN

DESK DRAWER (SPARE WEDDING RING, ETC)

STICKS OF VARIOUS KINDS

RADIO MICROPHONES

VERGER'S CERTIFICATE

VERGE, IN CABINET

KEY CUPBOARD

CUPBOARD FOR KEY-CUPBOARD KEY

GOWN

RAMPS, ROPES, ETC

LINEN LIBRARY

MIC NOT WORKING

TIME TO END SERMON

INTERCESSOR DOWN

FOLLOW ME

DRINKABLE COFFEE

GIN

PREACHERS' WATER

CORRECT PROCEDURES

WHAT TO DO IF THERE IS AN...

ACCIDENT

STRAY THURIBLE
WE WERE PROCESSING
AND THEN

WRITE IT IN THE 'ACCIDENTS' BOOK

INCIDENT

NO TEA BAGS
IT WAS TIME TO
BUT THEN

WRITE IT IN THE 'INCIDENTS' BOOK

AWKWARD SCENARIO

INTERCESSIONS MIXUP
THE ROTA CLEARLY
HOWEVER

WRITE IT IN THE 'AWKWARD SCENARIOS' BOOK

EMBARRASSING MOMENT

RADIO MICROPHONE
THE VICAR WAS IN
WE HEARD

WRITE IT IN THE 'EMBARRASSING MOMENTS' BOOK

SIMPLIFICATION

A TASK GROUP HAS BEEN AT WORK IN THE PARISH

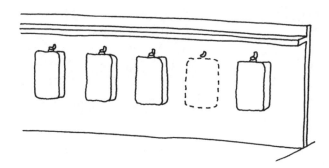

HASSOCK CUTBACKS

A STREAMLINED PCC

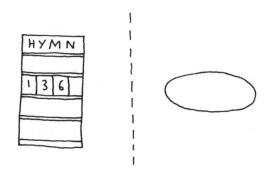

NOT SO MANY HYMNS. OR BISCUITS

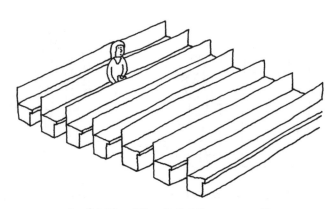

A REDUCED CONGREGATION

THANKLESS TASKS

ANSWERING THE DOOR AT
ALL HOURS AND FOR
VARIOUS REASONS

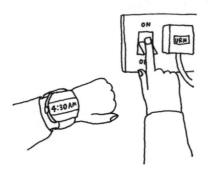

TURNING ON
THE URN

PICKING UP PIECES OF
GLITTER ONE BY ONE

TESTING THE WATER IN
THE PREACHERS' GLASS

ENCOURAGING YOUNG PEOPLE TO
FIND A DIFFERENT WALL TO
KICK A FOOTBALL AGAINST

DISPOSING OF THINGS
DISCOVERED IN THE CHURCHYARD

HEALTH AND SAFETY

GUIDANCE FOR CHURCHES: THINGS YOU NEED TO DO

RISK ASSESSMENTS
BEFORE EACH SERVICE

HI-VIS JACKETS
FOR SIDESPERSONS

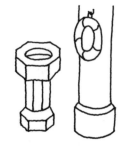

A LIFEBELT
NEXT TO
THE FONT

PADDED BUFFERS ON
PEW-ENDS FOR CHILDREN
CAREERING AROUND THE
AISLES AT HIGH SPEED

HARD HATS
FOR ANYONE
CARRYING
A STICK

GLOVES TO BE USED BY
ALL BISCUIT-ARRANGERS

A SERVER TO TRY THE
COMMUNION WINE
IN THE VESTRY
(IN CASE POISONED)

PARACHUTE FOR
EMERGENCY
DESCENT FROM
ORGAN LOFT

THE TALENT POOL

MEMBERS OF THE CONGREGATION WHO HAVE BEEN SPECIALLY SELECTED TO GO ON TO GREATER THINGS

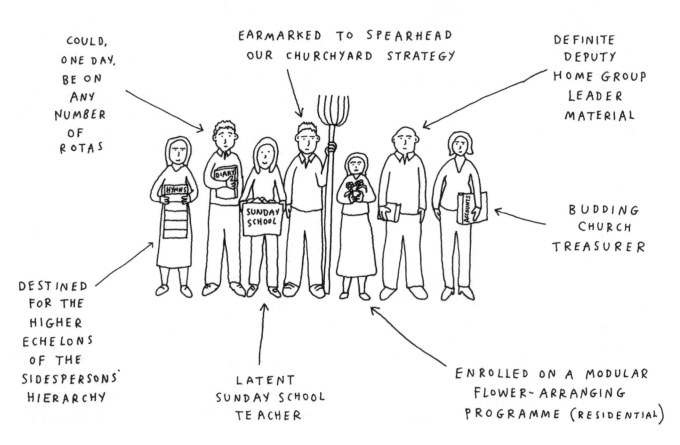

COULD, ONE DAY, BE ON ANY NUMBER OF ROTAS

EARMARKED TO SPEARHEAD OUR CHURCHYARD STRATEGY

DEFINITE DEPUTY HOME GROUP LEADER MATERIAL

BUDDING CHURCH TREASURER

DESTINED FOR THE HIGHER ECHELONS OF THE SIDESPERSONS' HIERARCHY

LATENT SUNDAY SCHOOL TEACHER

ENROLLED ON A MODULAR FLOWER-ARRANGING PROGRAMME (RESIDENTIAL)

NEW YEAR'S RESOLUTIONS

HOW THE CHURCH CAN HELP

EXERCISE

MEETING NEW PEOPLE

HEALTHY EATING

GETTING ORGANISED

AT THE PCC WE'LL DISCUSS THE APCM, CW VS THE BCP, THE LLM'S CRB, AND THE OLM'S BAP. OH, AND THERE ARE LETTERS FROM THE DAC, THE DDO, THE HOB AND THE ABC

LEARNING A NEW LANGUAGE

TRAVELLING TO NEW PLACES

OBSERVING LENT

LESS DEMANDING OPTIONS

WINE   CHOCOLATE   SPROUTS
                     LIVER
                     SPAM
                     YEAST EXTRACT

CHOOSE ITEMS TO GIVE UP CAREFULLY

SCREEN 2

TAKE A LENT COURSE BASED AROUND
WATCHING ONE OR MORE FILMS

ALLOW SUNDAYS AS 'FEAST DAYS'

PUB

DECIDE THAT SUNDAY STARTS AFTER
EVENING PRAYER ON SATURDAY

LENT

MODERN-DAY SACRIFICES

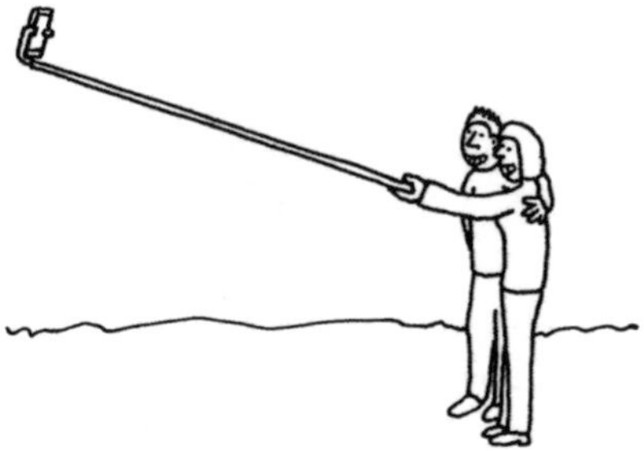

GIVING UP SELFIES

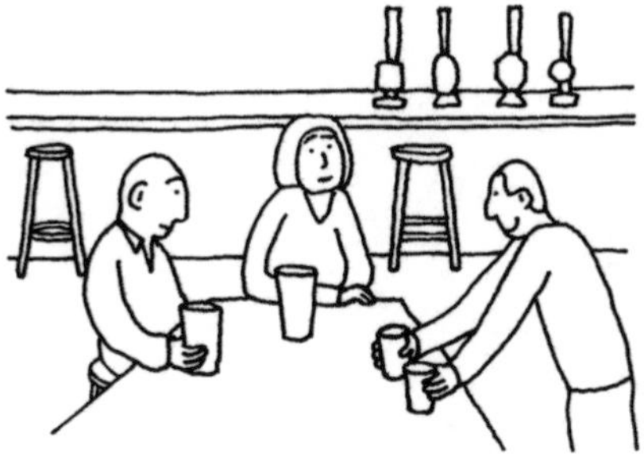

STICKING TO HALF PINTS

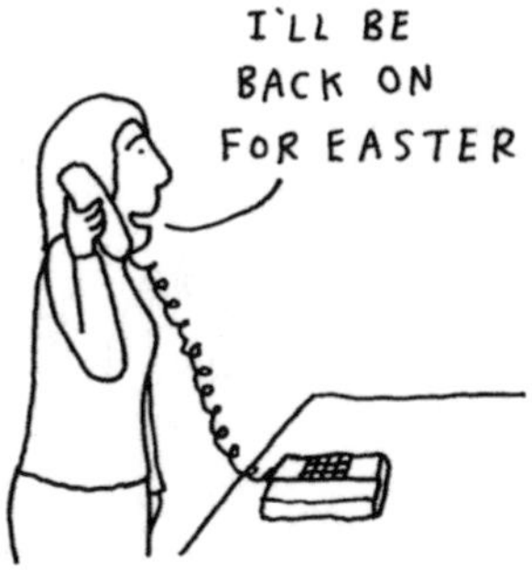
I'LL BE BACK ON FOR EASTER

TAKING A BREAK FROM THE FLOWER ROTA

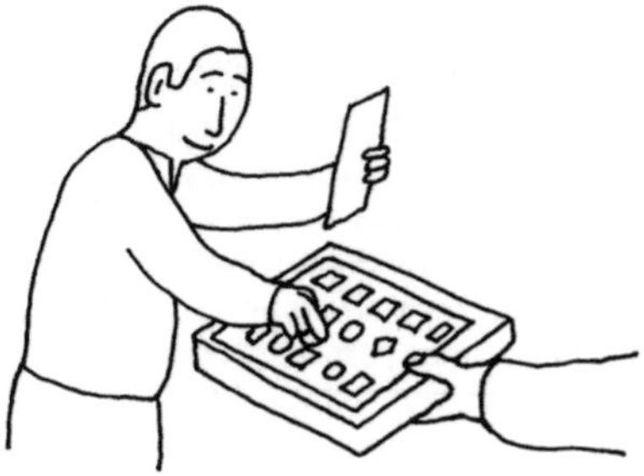

STEERING CLEAR OF COFFEE CREAMS IN SELECTION BOXES

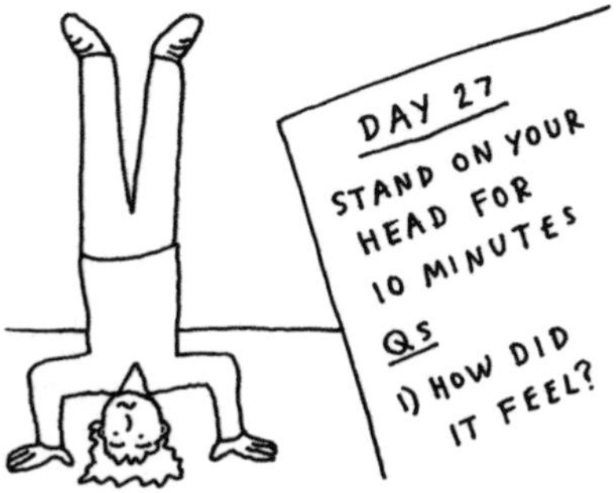
DAY 27
STAND ON YOUR HEAD FOR 10 MINUTES
QS
1) HOW DID IT FEEL?

USING PUBLISHED LENT RESOURCES

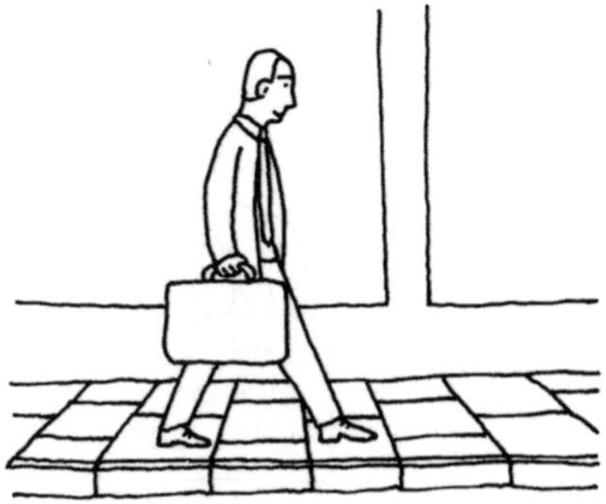

AVOIDING THE CRACKS IN THE PAVEMENT

CHANGING THE DATE OF EASTER

THINGS LIKELY TO BE RESOLVED BEFORE IT HAPPENS

ENGLAND WINNING THE WORLD CUP

A VERIFIABLE SIGHTING OF THE LOCH NESS MONSTER

THE PUBLICATION OF THE CHILCOT REPORT

GETTING THE CHURCH NOTICE BOARD UP TO DATE

THE SUMMER

EARLY MORNING SERVICES
BECOME POPULAR

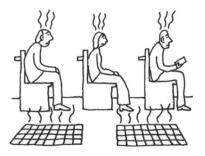

THE HEATING FINALLY
STARTS WORKING

A RELIEF CONGREGATION IS
BROUGHT IN TO COVER ABSENTEES

PARISH PICNICS
TAKE PLACE

THERE ARE NOT AS
MANY E-MAILS

MEMBERS OF THE CHURCH
SEND POSTCARDS

SUMMER HOLIDAYS

WHAT THE CONGREGATION DO WHEN THE CLERGY ARE AWAY

WHAT THE CLERGY DO WHEN THE CONGREGATION ARE AWAY

EXPLORE THE VESTRY

HAVE VERY SHORT SERMONS

REMOVE THE ROOD SCREEN

BURN THE OLD HYMN BOOKS

PLAY BOARD GAMES WHILST EATING ALL OF THE TASTY BISCUITS

CANCEL CHURCH, AND SIT IN THE RECTORY GARDEN, DRINKING PIMMS

NOT SO MUCH UNDERNEATH (YOU WILL HAVE TO BELIEVE ME)

DRESS DOWN

CANCEL CHURCH, AND SIT IN THE RECTORY GARDEN, DRINKING PIMMS

THE SUMMER FESTIVAL

HOW TO SPOT MEMBERS OF THE CONGREGATION WHO HAVE BEEN

MUDDY
BOOTS

ANY VOLUNTEERS?

UNEXPECTED BURSTS
OF ENTHUSIASM

SUMMER FESTIVAL

NEW
T-SHIRTS

A LOT OF
LAUNDRY

WE'VE ALREADY
TRIED IT

BRILLIANT
IDEAS

FOOD
DONATIONS

A SURPLUS OF VARIOUS ITEMS OF
FOOD, WHICH TURNED OUT NOT
TO BE NEEDED ONCE IT WAS
DISCOVERED THAT THERE WAS A
VAN SELLING BACON SANDWICHES

THE SUMMER FESTIVAL

TIPS FOR TRAVELLING LIGHT

CUT EXCESS
MATERIAL FROM
WELLIES

THE TENT WILL STILL
STAND UP WITH
FEWER PEGS

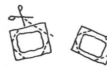

TRIM CORNERS FROM
RECTANGULAR
TEA BAGS

TOOTHBRUSH HANDLE:
UNNECESSARY

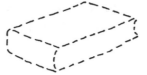

REFERENCE BOOKS:
LEAVE BEHIND

FILL GAPS IN CASE
WITH HELIUM BALLOONS

TENT
ROTA
Fri
Sat
Sun
Mon

SHARE CAMPING EQUIPMENT

EMOTIONAL BAGGAGE.
REDUCE IF POSSIBLE
(TRY COMPRESSING
WITH A BUNGEE)

EAT/DRINK PROVISIONS
BEFORE ARRIVING

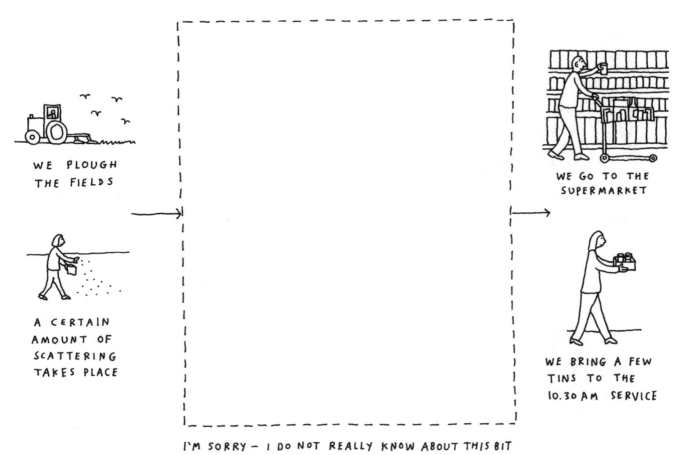

HARVEST

HOW WE GET OUR FOOD

WE PLOUGH
THE FIELDS

A CERTAIN
AMOUNT OF
SCATTERING
TAKES PLACE

WE GO TO THE
SUPERMARKET

WE BRING A FEW
TINS TO THE
10.30 AM SERVICE

I'M SORRY — I DO NOT REALLY KNOW ABOUT THIS BIT

ADVENT
HAZARDS

TABLES BUCKLING UNDER SHEER
WEIGHT OF MINCE PIES

UNREST OVER THE CORRECT WEEK
TO LIGHT THE PINK CANDLE

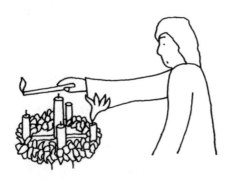

ADVENT WREATH FIRES

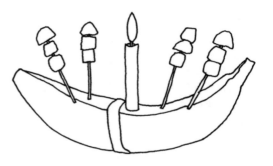

SUPERMARKETS RUNNING OUT
OF ORANGES

DELIVERIES

TO THE VICARAGE ON A TYPICAL DECEMBER DAY

THE PARISH CHRISTMAS TREE

PARCEL FOR NO 43

CHRISTMAS SERVICE SUPPLIES

THE CHRISTMAS SHOPPING

COURIER ARRIVING
DURING THE SCHOOL RUN

PARISHIONER WITH CARD
ATTEMPTING TO AVOID DETECTION

THE CHRISTMAS DECORATIONS

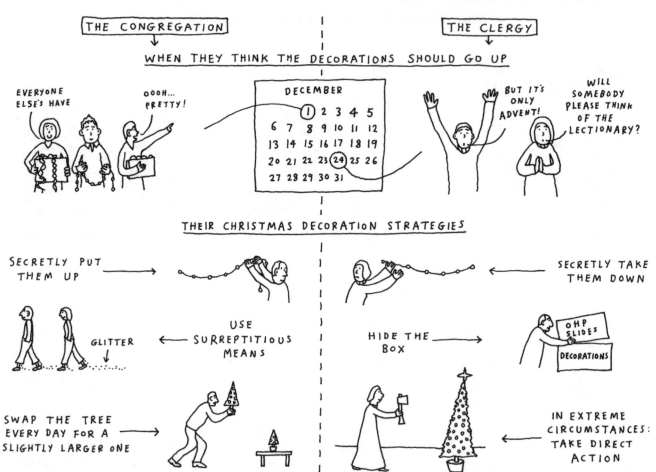

THE NATIVITY PLAY
PEDANTIC / SCHOLARLY VERSION

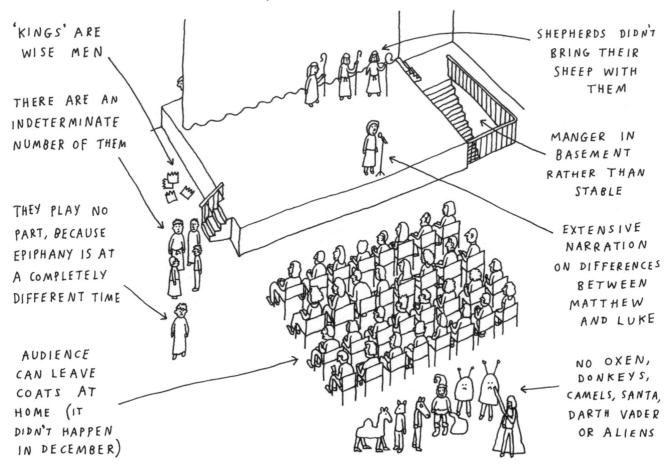

'KINGS' ARE WISE MEN

THERE ARE AN INDETERMINATE NUMBER OF THEM

THEY PLAY NO PART, BECAUSE EPIPHANY IS AT A COMPLETELY DIFFERENT TIME

AUDIENCE CAN LEAVE COATS AT HOME (IT DIDN'T HAPPEN IN DECEMBER)

SHEPHERDS DIDN'T BRING THEIR SHEEP WITH THEM

MANGER IN BASEMENT RATHER THAN STABLE

EXTENSIVE NARRATION ON DIFFERENCES BETWEEN MATTHEW AND LUKE

NO OXEN, DONKEYS, CAMELS, SANTA, DARTH VADER OR ALIENS

73

CHRISTMAS CHURCHGOERS

HOW TO GET THEM TO ATTEND THE REST OF THE YEAR

1 GIVE THEM A WELCOME PACK

FASCINATING LEAFLETS ← EXPLAINING EVERYTHING

SERVICE TIMES

SOME CHOCOLATE

2 INSPIRE THEM

PICTURE OF SERMON TO GIVE GENERAL IDEA →

3 CATCH THEM DURING A MOMENT OF WEAKNESS

ROTA

4 MAKE IT INCREDIBLY DIFFICULT TO LEAVE

WELCOME
EXIT ONLY
← WAY IN

MAJOR SPORTING EVENTS

SIGNS THAT THE CONGREGATION ARE BEING DISTRACTED

WE USE THEM TO FOLLOW
THE BIBLE READINGS

AN INCREASE IN THE NUMBER
OF MOBILE DEVICES

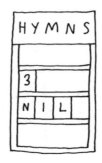

UNEXPECTED AMENDMENTS
TO THE HYMN BOARDS

THE APPEARANCE OF
UNEXPLAINED WIRES

AN UPSURGE IN INTEREST
IN THE CHURCH WIFI CODE

CHEERING AT POINTS WHERE
THE LITURGY DOES NOT
INDICATE CHEERING

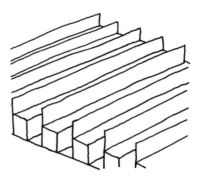

NO ONE IS THERE

FOOTBALL

LESSONS THE CHURCH COULD LEARN

"NEXT WEEK'S SERVICE WON'T BE THAT INTERESTING"

TRY TO AVOID OWN GOALS

THE OFFSIDE RULE

IT IS IMPORTANT TO EXPLAIN THE REGULATIONS

I HARDLY TOUCHED HIM

IT IS ACCEPTABLE TO EXAGGERATE INJURIES

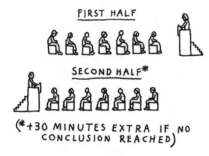

FIRST HALF

SECOND HALF*

(*+30 MINUTES EXTRA IF NO CONCLUSION REACHED)

CHANGING ENDS AT HALF TIME ADDS VARIETY

CHURCH EXPERT BLOG

PUNDITS DON'T ALWAYS KNOW WHAT THEY ARE TALKING ABOUT

CHANTING

TRAVELLING GREAT DISTANCES

WEARING THE KIT

CHURCH STICKERS

STICKER ALBUMS

IT IS GOOD TO DEMONSTRATE ENTHUSIASM

CYCLING

IDEAS FOR CHURCHGOERS

THE AERO-BIRETTA

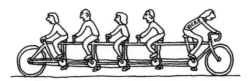

BICYCLE FOR SMALL CONGREGATIONS

PADDED GLOVES FOR HOLDING HYMN BOOK DURING LENGTHY HYMNS

PADDED TROUSERS FOR WOODEN PEWS

BELL

NOT SHOWN: THE ANGLICAN CYCLE OF PRAYER

LITURGICALLY-CORRECT HANDLEBAR STREAMERS

SKIN TIGHT CLERGY SHIRT

AN ECHELON OF SIDESPERSONS

PREACHING BICYCLE

KNEELER WITH BICYCLE ON IT

THE TOUR DE FRANCE
WAYS THE CHURCH COULD DRAW INSPIRATION

HANDING OUT REFRESHMENTS
ON THE MOVE

BECOMING MORE
AERODYNAMIC

WEARING HELMETS (ESPECIALLY
WHEN THERE ARE HAZARDS)

ASSEMBLING FOR A STRATEGY
DISCUSSION ON THE TEAM BUS

GIVING WINNERS THEIR MOMENT
OF GLORY ON THE PODIUM

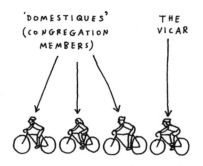

EVERYBODY WORKING FOR
THE TEAM LEADER

RAFFLE PRIZES

GIFT BOX OF
TOILETRIES FROM
LAST CHRISTMAS

POTTED
PLANT
(ALWAYS A
BEGONIA)

HALF AN HOUR OF
A CONGREGATION
MEMBER'S TIME

HIGHLY IMPRACTICAL
CUDDLY TOY
(NO SPACE TO
SHOW IT ALL)

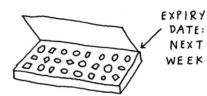

EXPIRY
DATE:
NEXT
WEEK

BOX OF
CHOCOLATES

SCENTED
CANDLE

BOTTLE OF
LIQUEUR
(HAS BEEN A
RAFFLE PRIZE
SEVEN TIMES
ALREADY)

1987

VINTAGE
CALENDAR

UNWANTED
APPLIANCE

10000 PIECES

JIGSAW

VOUCHER

CLIMB
THE
CHURCH
TOWER

VOUCHER FOR
RELIGIOUS
EXPERIENCE

THE QUIZ NIGHT

THE TEAMS, AND THEIR SPECIALIST SUBJECTS

QUIZMASTER

THE SUNDAY SCHOOL TEACHERS

(ART, DRAMA)

THE CHOIR

(HYMNS, ANTHEMS)

THE FLOWER LADIES

(FLOWERS, FOLIAGE, HORROR FILMS)

THE P.C.C.

(POLITICS, MAJOR CONFLICTS)

MEMBERS OF THE GENERAL CONGREGATION

(GENERAL KNOWLEDGE)

TRAVELLING QUIZ EXPERTS

(GEOGRAPHY, ARTS & LITERATURE, ENTERTAINMENT, SPORTS & LEISURE, SCIENCE & NATURE, HISTORY)

THE SIDESPERSONS

(CURRENCY, GEOGRAPHY, SHEEPDOG TRIALS)

THE CLERGY

(THE BIBLE, THE HOLY LAND, TRAINS)

THE CHURCH FETE

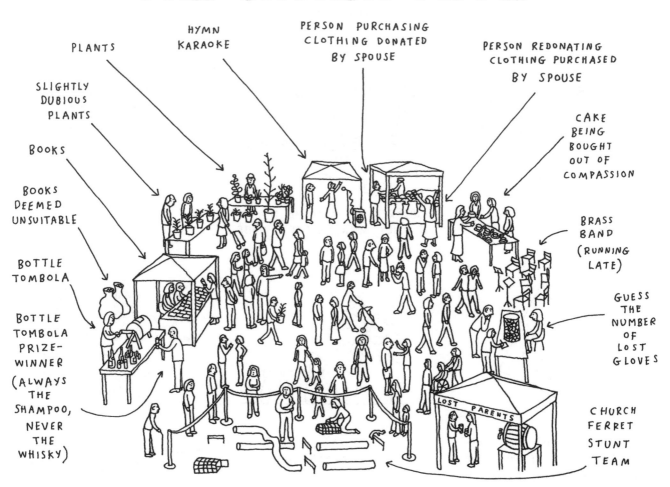

PLANTS

HYMN KARAOKE

PERSON PURCHASING CLOTHING DONATED BY SPOUSE

PERSON REDONATING CLOTHING PURCHASED BY SPOUSE

SLIGHTLY DUBIOUS PLANTS

CAKE BEING BOUGHT OUT OF COMPASSION

BOOKS

BOOKS DEEMED UNSUITABLE

BRASS BAND (RUNNING LATE)

BOTTLE TOMBOLA

GUESS THE NUMBER OF LOST GLOVES

BOTTLE TOMBOLA PRIZE-WINNER (ALWAYS THE SHAMPOO, NEVER THE WHISKY)

LOST PARENTS

CHURCH FERRET STUNT TEAM

THE WEDDING SERVICE

INSTRUCTIONS FOR GUESTS

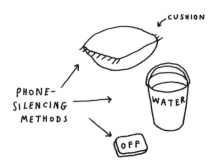

PLEASE SILENCE
YOUR PHONE

CHILDREN ARE WELCOME. IT'S OK
IF THEY MAKE A BIT OF NOISE

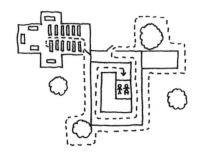

TOILETS ARE IN
THE CHURCH HALL

IF YOU WOULD LIKE TO MAKE
A DONATION TO THE CHURCH WE
HAVE SOME SPECIAL ENVELOPES

NO FLASHING

PLEASE KEEP CONFETTI WITHIN
THE DESIGNATED AREA

GETTING MARRIED

QUALIFYING CONNECTIONS FOR BEING MARRIED IN A PARTICULAR CHURCH

LIVED IN PARISH
FOR SIX MONTHS

GONE TO THE CHURCH
FOR SIX MONTHS

HAVING THE RECEPTION
IN PUB NEXT DOOR

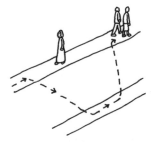

FALLEN OUT WITH VICAR
IN THE CHURCH
DOWN THE ROAD

PARENTS LIVE IN
PARISH OR HAVE
OWN PEW

GRANDPARENTS
WERE MARRIED
THERE

NEED A PRETTY CHURCH
FOR THE PICTURES

DRESS STYLE MATCHES
THE ARCHITECTURE

<u>OK</u>

<u>THE CUT-OFF
LINE</u>

<u>NOT OK</u>

UNITY

VARIOUS OBSERVATIONS

LITURGICAL
DIFFERENCES
ARE BEST
SETTLED
BY MEANS
OF A DUEL →

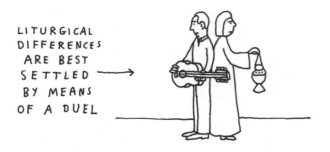

EVERYONE
IS WELCOME
AT THE
ECUMENICAL
SERVICE ←

HOME → WORSHIPPERS
← AWAY WORSHIPPERS

A FEW PEOPLE MAY WALK OUT

↑
DEEPLY
OFFENDED

↑
FELT
IGNORED

↑
PUTTING EXTRA
MONEY INTO
PARKING METER

↑

ONLOOKERS CONTINUE TO BE UTTERLY BAFFLED
BY THE FACT THAT, GIVEN EVERYTHING ELSE
CURRENTLY GOING ON IN THE WORLD, SO MUCH
ENERGY IS TAKEN UP BY DISPUTES OVER SEXUALITY

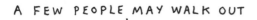

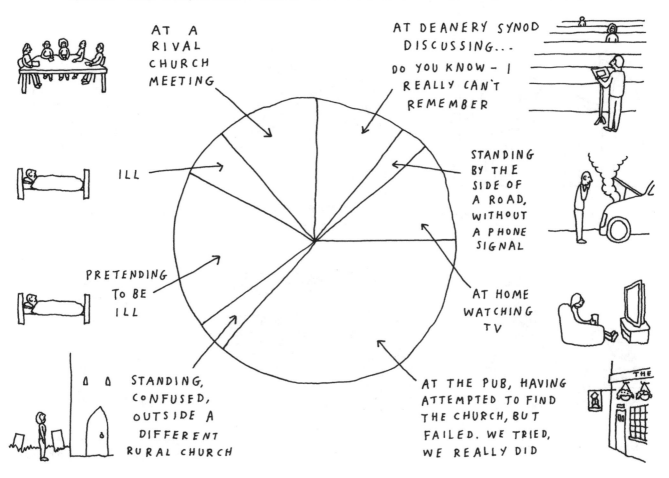

THE DEANERY SYNOD

WHERE THE MEMBERS WERE AT THE TIME OF THE MEETING

AT A RIVAL CHURCH MEETING

AT DEANERY SYNOD DISCUSSING...
DO YOU KNOW - I REALLY CAN'T REMEMBER

ILL

STANDING BY THE SIDE OF A ROAD, WITHOUT A PHONE SIGNAL

PRETENDING TO BE ILL

AT HOME WATCHING TV

STANDING, CONFUSED, OUTSIDE A DIFFERENT RURAL CHURCH

AT THE PUB, HAVING ATTEMPTED TO FIND THE CHURCH, BUT FAILED. WE TRIED, WE REALLY DID

THEOLOGICAL STUDENTS

EXPLAIN HOW THEY SPENT THEIR SUMMER

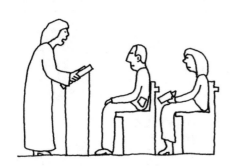

SALLY: HONING PREACHING SKILLS

PAUL: UNDERTAKING A MISSIONARY JOURNEY

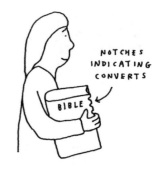

ELAINE: EVANGELISING

HENRY: GOING TO FESTIVALS

FELICITY: WORKING

JOHN: CONTEMPLATING GOD'S CELESTIAL CREATION

BISHOPS

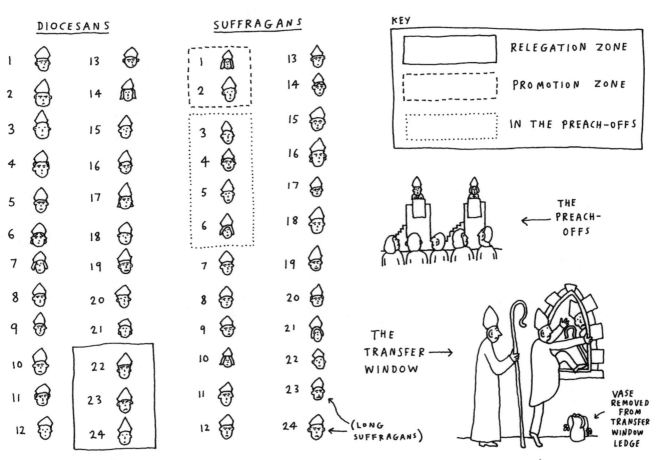

DIOCESANS

1, 2, 3, 4, 5, 6, 7, 8, 9, 10, 11, 12, 13, 14, 15, 16, 17, 18, 19, 20, 21, 22, 23, 24

SUFFRAGANS

1, 2, 3, 4, 5, 6, 7, 8, 9, 10, 11, 12, 13, 14, 15, 16, 17, 18, 19, 20, 21, 22, 23, 24 (LONG SUFFRAGANS)

KEY

RELEGATION ZONE

PROMOTION ZONE

IN THE PREACH-OFFS

THE PREACH-OFFS

THE TRANSFER WINDOW

VASE REMOVED FROM TRANSFER WINDOW LEDGE

(PRECISE NUMBERS OF BISHOPS NOT CORRECT AS I HAVE MADE THEM UP)

THE ARCHBISHOP

MEMBERS OF HIS ENTOURAGE

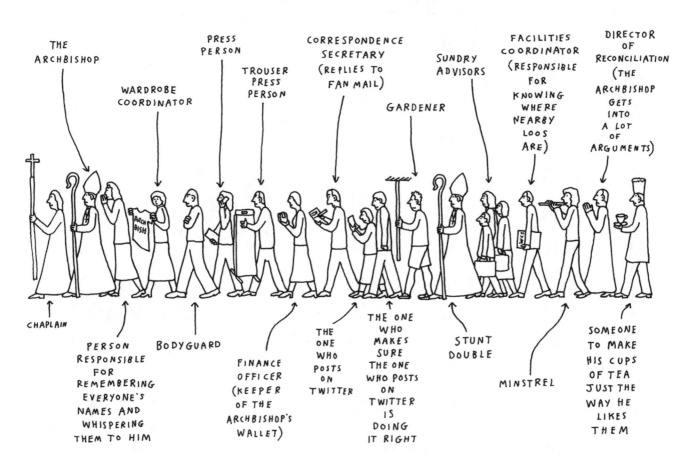

HOW TO FIND US

ON FOOT

FOLLOW THE TRAIL
OF CONFETTI

BY PUBLIC TRANSPORT

THE RAIL-REPLACEMENT
BUS SERVICE PASSES BY (BUT
DOESN'T STOP) ON SUNDAYS

BY ROAD (USING SAT NAV)

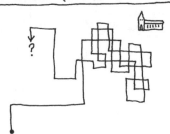

GOOD LUCK

BY BICYCLE

PLEASE LET US KNOW IF YOU ARE
CONSIDERING THIS. PERHAPS THE
DIOCESE HAS MONEY FOR BIKE RACKS

BY BOAT

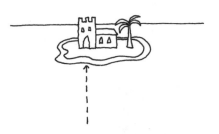

NAVIGATE IN
DIRECTION SHOWN

PARKING INFORMATION

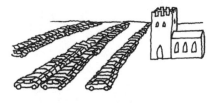

ARRIVE EARLY TO GET A
SPACE. SOME OF US HAVE TO
DRIVE OVER HALF A MILE

ANY OTHER BUSINESS

PLEASE
LEAVE
KITCHEN
TIDY

NIGEL
SAID
HE'S
LEAVING

NEED
LOTS
MORE
HELPERS

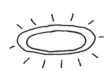

WHERE
IS
MY
PLATTER?

SOME
HYMNS
ARE
UNKNOWN

THAT
ISN'T
YOUR
CUPBOARD

KIDS
MADE
SOME
NOISE

WHEN
IS
THE
FETE?

CAN
WE
BAN
SKATEBOARDS?

I
HATE
THE
COFFEE

CHURCHYARD
IS
LOOKING
UNKEMPT

NO
PROGRESS
ON
WIFI

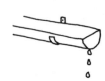

QUOTE
NEEDED
FOR
GUTTERING

CROCKERY
HAS
GONE
MISSING

MICE
LIVE
IN
VESTRY

YOUTHS
BROKE
TODDLER
TOYS

WHOSE
IS
THAT
UMBRELLA?

HAS
ANYONE
SEEN
ELSIE?